CENTRAL OFFICE OF INFORMATION REFERENCE PAMPHLET **178**

Organisation of Political Parties in Britain

LONDON HER MAJESTY'S STATIONERY OFFICE

Organisation of Political Parties in Britain

LONDON

HER MAJESTY'S STATIONERY OFFICE

Prepared by

Reference Services, Publications Division

Central Office of Information, London

© Crown copyright 1983

First published 1983

329.942
G7860

ISBN 0 11 701043 X
84-2530

Contents

Introduction   1

Historical Background   2

Recent Developments   4

The Party System   6

Party Organisation Outside Parliament   8

Party Organisation Inside Parliament   20

The Nationalist Parties: Scottish National Party
and Plaid Cymru   23

Northern Ireland Parties   25

Appendices

    1: Principal Minor Parties   30

    2: General Election Results 1970–79   31

Party Addresses   32

Reading List   33

Introduction

The British system of parliamentary democracy is based on the party system in which office is sought by organised political parties able to form and support a stable government. The party system itself rests on the assumption that there are at least two parties in the House of Commons, each of which is sufficiently united on matters of policy and principle to be able to form a government at any time.[1] The parties are not registered or formally recognised in law, but in practice most candidates in elections, and almost all winning candidates, belong to one of the main political parties.

Much public interest has recently been shown in the emergence in 1981 of a new political party—the Social Democratic Party—and its formation of an electoral alliance with the Liberal Party; and in the effect this may have on what has been, since 1945, basically a two-party system.

After a brief historical background of the origins of the major political parties and an outline of the modern party system, this pamphlet describes the organisation—both inside and outside Parliament—of the Conservative, Labour, Liberal, and Social Democratic parties. The organisation of the two nationalist parties—the Scottish National Party and Plaid Cymru (Welsh Nationalist Party)—and that of the main political parties in Northern Ireland—Official Unionist, Democratic Unionist, Social Democratic and Labour, and Alliance—is considered in separate chapters.

---

[1] *For further details see COI reference pamphlet* The British Parliament, *No 56/RP/80.*

Historical Background

For the last 150 years British parliamentary democracy has been based on a predominantly two-party system: with first Whigs and Tories, then Liberals and Conservatives, and most recently Labour and Conservatives alternating in power.[1]

Associations of like-minded people are inevitable in any organised society when the principles and practices of government are open to public debate and discussion. In England they have existed in one form or another at least since medieval times. Yet for centuries, and long after the real power in the State had passed from the Crown to Parliament, such associations were loosely knit and impermanent, being formed for the most part to achieve some particular purpose, and afterwards dissolving and regrouping for some other cause. The origins of organised political parties in Britain[2] are comparatively recent: before 1832—the date of the first parliamentary Reform Act— there was no clear-cut division in the House of Commons along modern party lines. The terms 'Whig' and 'Tory' to describe certain political leanings had then been in use for about 150 years, but there was no party organisation of any sort outside Parliament; even within Parliament there existed no strong party discipline.

The reason for this lack of cohesion lay, to a great extent, in the comparatively small size and exclusive nature of the electorate. In 1830 there were 656 Members of Parliament (MPs) in the House of Commons, rather more than there are today, but they were returned by an electorate of only about 500,000 out of a total adult population of some 10 million. Many of the growing industrial areas had no representation in Parliament, while ancient country towns sometimes returned two members. The outcome of elections was decided by a small number of influential citizens, and not by the public at large. The personal influence of a candidate counted for more than the policy of a party; and once an MP had been elected, he was under no obligation to follow a party line.

The growth of the modern party system was brought about by parliamentary reform and the gradual extension of voting rights to the whole adult population.[3] As corrupt election practices were gradually eliminated, as representation in Parliament became more equitably distributed throughout the country, and as the social composition of the electorate changed, it became difficult for a candidate to offer himself as an individual to the voters. Politicians, as the representatives of millions of newly enfranchised voters, began to form coherent parties pledged to carry out definite policies based on principles which their supporters were prepared to endorse.

In these circumstances it became obvious that some form of political organisation outside Parliament, as well as within it, was essential if votes were to be won and support maintained. The first organised political parties on the modern pattern—the Conservative and Liberal parties—were, broadly speaking, successors to the Tories and Whigs of the eighteenth and early nineteenth centuries. The word 'Conservative'

---

[1]   *This is reflected in the layout of the House of Commons chamber, which is rectangular, with benches ranged opposite each other, and with supporters of the Government sitting on one side, opposition members on the other. This contrasts with many other national legislatures in which the seats are arranged in circular fashion.*

[2]   *The term 'Britain' is used informally in this pamphlet to mean the United Kingdom of Great Britain and Northern Ireland; 'Great Britain' comprises England, Wales and Scotland.*

[3]   *The franchise was extended by legislation in 1832, 1867, 1884, 1918, and 1928. In 1969 the voting age was reduced from 21 to 18.*

in its modern political sense first came into use after about 1830 and gradually became a normal expression to describe the successors of the Tories. The Liberal Party was formed towards the end of the 1850s with the support of former Whigs and other political groups.

Both the Liberals and the Conservatives created national headquarters in the 1860s. The Liberal Party central organisation began in 1860 when some Liberal MPs established the Liberal Registration Association, designed to encourage the registration of voters and to foster the growth of constituency associations. Further steps to strengthen Liberal organisations came after a heavy defeat of the Party in the 1874 general election; in 1877 a large meeting in Birmingham (then the centre of Joseph Chamberlain's successful Liberal association) established the National Liberal Federation, which was charged with forming Liberal constituency associations. Under the Federation's rules, affiliated associations could send representatives to an annual meeting of the Federation's council, a forerunner of the annual party conference.

The Conservative Party founded the National Union of Conservative and Constitutional Associations in 1867, the year of the second Reform Act which considerably enlarged the number of voters able to take part in a parliamentary election. The National Union became the national organisation of the Conservative constituency associations designed to increase popular support for the Party outside Parliament. After the Conservative defeat in the 1868 general election, the Party, under the leadership of Benjamin Disraeli, created the Conservative Central Office to encourage the organisation of constituency associations and to keep a register of candidates for elections.

As the number of voters increased, a third party came into existence with the aim of representing working men in Parliament. As with the Liberal Party 50 to 60 years earlier, the formation of the Labour Party was the product both of a new body of voters created by legislation and of the growth of a new ideology.

Unlike the earlier parties, which began as parliamentary groups *within* Parliament and which established organisations outside it in order to enlist support and so facilitate re-election, the Labour Party began as a movement *outside* Parliament, seeking representation within in order to further the aims of party policy. In 1893 an Independent Labour Party was formed in Bradford and, following a meeting in 1900 with some trade unions and socialist societies, a Labour Representation Committee was established to co-ordinate plans for Labour representation in Parliament. After the 1906 election the Committee became the Labour Party. Local committees were established at constituency level, but there was no individual membership, the Committee consisting entirely of affiliated organisations. In 1918 the Party was completely reorganised, constituency Labour parties admitting individual members as well as affiliated organisations.

During the inter-war period (1918–39) the Labour Party supplanted the Liberal Party, which last formed a government by itself in 1906–16, as the main rival of the Conservative Party. The first Labour Government held office as a minority government for ten months of 1924, and in 1929–31 the Party took office for a second time, again as a minority government. Since 1945 there have been five Conservative and six Labour Governments and almost all the members of the House of Commons have represented either the Conservative or the Labour Party. Despite its considerable electoral strength in the country (see p 5), the Liberal Party has not, since 1945, had more than 15 members in the House of Commons at any one time.

Recent Developments

A notable feature of the parliamentary party system during the last eight years has been the increase in the representation of smaller parties in the House of Commons. Thus the Liberal Party, which in the 1970 general election had secured only six seats, returned 14 in the first, and 13 in the second of the two 1974 elections. Moreover, the nationalist parties in Scotland and Wales also made considerable advances in 1974: the Scottish National Party (SNP) returned seven members in the February election, and 11 in October. Plaid Cymru, the Welsh Nationalist Party (literally, 'The Party of Wales'), returned two and three MPs in the two contests.

In the 1979 general election, however, all minor parties, outside Northern Ireland, lost the ground gained earlier: the Conservative Party was returned to power with an overall majority of 43 seats—the first clear-cut parliamentary majority for either major party since 1970, and the representation of third parties, outside Northern Ireland, was greatly reduced. The Liberals were reduced from 14 to 11, the SNP from 11 to 2, and Plaid Cymru from 3 to 2, while the Scottish Labour Party with 2 MPs[1] disappeared from the House of Commons altogether, confirming the increasing volatility of the British electorate which has been a feature of recent elections.

The SNP had been formed in 1934 from among supporters of self-government for Scotland and returned its first MP in a by-election in 1945. It subsequently lost support; but during the 1960s its membership increased and it secured a by-election success in 1967, and in 1970 won its first seat at a general election. Like the SNP, Plaid Cymru made considerable advances in membership during the 1960s. Founded in 1925, it secured its first seat in the House of Commons at a by-election in 1966, but although it contested, for the first time, all 36 Welsh seats in the 1970 general election, it failed to return any members to the House of Commons.

A new political party appeared in March 1981 when a number of Labour MPs, two former Labour ministers, not then in Parliament, and one Conservative MP broke away from their parties to form the Social Democratic Party (SDP).

At the time of its launch, the parliamentary group of the SDP consisted of 14 MPs—13 former Labour and one former Conservative—who had resigned from their parties to join the Council for Social Democracy, set up in January 1981 to 'rally all those . . . committed to the values, principles and policies of social democracy'. The Council was set up as a result of disagreement with the Labour Party's approach to a number of issues and procedures. The new Party is now represented in the House of Commons by 30 MPs.

The SDP has entered into an alliance with the Liberal Party to contest the next general election. Since October 1981, three MPs—one Liberal and two SDP—have been directly elected as Alliance candidates. While the Liberal Party and the SDP are two distinct parties, they share a common approach to major policy issues and a commitment to break up the established two-party system.

---

[1] *The Scottish Labour Party was formed in January 1976. Two Labour Party MPs who joined it retained the Labour Party whip in the House of Commons until July 1976 when they indicated that the Scottish Labour Party would act as an independent party within Parliament.*

Present State of the Parties

At the last general election in May 1979 all but 28 of the 635 Members of Parliament were elected as Conservative or Labour (see Appendix 2, p 31); the Liberal Party had 11 members; the Scottish National Party 2; Plaid Cymru (Welsh Nationalists) 2; the Official Unionist Party (Northern Ireland) 5; Democratic Unionist Party (Northern Ireland) 3; and other Northern Ireland political groups 4.

The Speaker, who presides over the debates of the House of Commons, was elected as 'the Speaker seeking re-election' (see footnote, p 31). A number of by-elections and other changes have subsequently altered the strength of the parties so that in January 1983 seats were distributed as follows:

Conservative	333
Labour	239
Social Democratic	30
Liberal	12
Scottish National	2
Plaid Cymru (Welsh Nationalist)	2
Official Unionist (Northern Ireland)	5
Democratic Unionist (Northern Ireland)	3
United Ulster Unionist (Northern Ireland)	1
Ulster Popular Unionist* (Northern Ireland)	1
Socialist (Northern Ireland)	1
Anti-H-Block Proxy Prisoner (Northern Ireland)	1
Vacant	1
TOTAL	631

*Formerly known as Ulster Progressive Unionist.

(In addition, there are the Speaker of the House of Commons and his three deputies —the Chairman of Ways and Means and the first and second Deputy Chairmen of Ways and Means. They do not vote except in their official capacities in the event of a tie.)

The total number of votes gained by the three main parties and their percentage of the total vote in the 1979 general election are given below.[1]

Party	Total vote	Percentage of total vote
Conservative	13,697,753	43·9
Labour	11,506,741	36·9
Liberal	4,305,324	13·8

[1] *Corresponding figures for the nationalist parties and the main parties in Northern Ireland appear on pp 23 and 25.*

The Party System

In the British electoral system the country is divided into 635 single-member constituencies, and representatives are elected to Parliament by the first-past-the-post (simple majority) method, which awards seats in the House of Commons to the candidates with the largest number of votes in a constituency, regardless of the size of that vote in relation to the total number of votes cast. The boundaries of the constituencies are reviewed at least every 15 years to take account of population changes. Under this system the strongest party in the House of Commons may have an absolute majority of seats with less than an absolute majority of votes. The system is generally considered to favour two-party competition, in particular competition between parties whose support is concentrated geographically, and to discriminate against parties with support distributed evenly across constituencies.[1]

Thus the party which wins most seats (though not necessarily the most votes), or which has the support of the majority of members in the House of Commons, usually forms the Government. The party with the next largest number of seats is officially recognised as 'Her Majesty's Opposition'; this has its own leader, who is paid a salary from public funds, and its own 'shadow cabinet'.[2] Members of other parties or any independents who have been elected support or oppose the Government according to their party or their own view of the policy being debated at any given time. Because the official Opposition is a minority party, it succeeds only infrequently in introducing or amending legislation; however, its pronouncements and policies are important since it is considered to be a potential Government—and would become so if successful at the next general election.

On occasion, a minority government may come into existence. This happens, for example, when no one party succeeds in winning a majority of seats over all the other parties combined (as after the general election of February 1974), or when, during the life of a Parliament, the governing party loses its majority through by-election defeats, as did the Labour Government in early 1977. In these circumstances, the Government has three choices: it may introduce only that legislation which commands the support of a majority in the House; it may make some form of arrangement with one or more opposition parties to enable it to stay in office; or it can ask for Parliament to be dissolved and for a general election to be held.

A minority government may stay in office so long as all other parties do not form a united parliamentary opposition to its policies and defeat it on a vote of confidence.

---

[1] *An alternative system of voting, that of proportional representation, which in various forms is used in most other Western countries in choosing their national legislatures, has been under discussion in political circles for a number of years. In the general election of May 1979, exact proportional representation, assuming identical votes had been cast, would have reduced the number of Conservative seats to 279 (compared with the 339 actually won), the number of Labour seats to 234 (compared with 268) and increased the number of Liberal seats to 88 (compared with the present 11). There would, therefore, have been no single party with an overall majority. The single transferable vote system of proportional representation is at present in use in Northern Ireland for European Parliament, Assembly and local government elections.*

[2] *For further details see COI reference paper* The Official Opposition in the British Parliament, *No 180/82.*

Occasionally, a minority administration has made a formal agreement with another party to support it. This occurred in March 1977 when the Labour Government made a formal agreement with the parliamentary Liberal Party whereby Liberal MPs agreed to 'work with the Government in the pursuit of economic recovery'. The 'Lib-Lab Pact', as it was called, lasted until the autumn of 1978 when Liberal support was withdrawn.

The formation of a coalition government in Britain has taken place during this century only for the sake of overcoming national crises, such as the two world wars or the economic depression during the 1930s. In a coalition, ministers are drawn from each of the parties concerned; the last coalition in Britain was dissolved in 1945 towards the end of the second world war.

The party system assumes that, in spite of the alternative programmes sponsored by the main political parties, there is common interest and agreement upon the maintenance of free institutions and parliamentary democracy.

Party Organisation Outside Parliament

This chapter deals with the organisation outside Parliament and with the office of party leader of the four main political parties at Westminster—Conservative, Labour, Liberal, and Social Democratic. The next chapter covers organisation inside Parliament. The two nationalist parties—the Scottish National Party and Plaid Cymru (Welsh Nationalist) —are considered on pp 23–4 and the main parties in Northern Ireland on pp 25–9.

Although there are important organisational differences, certain main elements are common to the general structure of each of the four main parties. Outside Parliament, the basic unit of organisation is the local *constituency association* (except for the SDP— see p 10), numbers of which are usually linked together in *regional federations*; also common to each party is a *national organisation* whose main function is to convene an *annual conference*, which provides a channel of communication between the leading members of the party in Parliament and their supporters in the country; and a *central office*, the national headquarters of the party, which is staffed by professional workers and provides a link between the party in Parliament and the party in the country. Finally there is the *leader of the party*. The roles of the party organisation and the importance of the annual party conference, however, vary between parties.

Constituency Associations or Parties

Outside Parliament, the basic unit in the structure of the main parties is the constituency association or party.

Conservative Party

Conservative constituency associations are composed of individual members, who live in or are connected with the constituency or have business interests there, and who subscribe annually to party funds. In many associations there are separate sections catering for the special interests of women; in almost all, there is a section for 'Young Conservatives' between the ages of 15 and 30. The Young Conservatives is the largest voluntary political youth movement in Britain and has branches in most parliamentary constituencies.

The associations have complete autonomy in the day-to-day management of their affairs: they are free to elect their own officers, select and appoint their own agents, raise their own funds, plan and carry out their own publicity programmes, conduct election campaigns in their constituencies in their own way, and adopt their own candidates for parliamentary and local government elections (the former from a list of names approved by the Party's Standing Advisory Committee on Candidates). There is a fairly wide variety in the structure of associations throughout the country, but in most of them the principal officers are the president, the chairman, three vice-chairmen (one man, one woman and one—male or female—Young Conservative) and the honorary treasurer. The governing body is normally the executive council, which is presided over by the chairman of the association and served by the agent in the capacity of secretary. The council deals with all matters affecting the association and it elects representatives to the national and area organisations. It also appoints, annually, a number of committees, including a finance and general purposes committee and those dealing with such subjects as political education, trade union affairs and local government.

In constituencies where the Conservative Party is highly organised, branches of the constituency association are set up in each ward or polling district for conducting normal constituency work. A number of local branch members are usually named as representatives from the branch to the executive council of the constituency association to act as a channel of communication between the branch and the association as a whole.

Labour Party

Labour constituency associations are known as Constituency Labour Parties (CLPs) within which branches may be formed, usually covering electoral wards in towns, and parishes or groups of parishes in rural areas. The associations have two classes of membership: affiliated organisations and individual members. *Affiliated organisations* include trade unions (the most important category); co-operative societies and branches of the Co-operative Party (the political wing of the Co-operative Movement—see p 30); branches of socialist societies or professional organisations which are affiliated to the Labour Party nationally; and trades councils. *Individual members* must be aged 15 years or over and must be attached to the appropriate branch operating in the area where they live or, for those of voting age, where they are registered as parliamentary or local government electors. They must accept and conform to the principles and policy of the Labour Party, and in addition they must, if eligible, belong to a trade union affiliated to the Trades Union Congress or to a union recognised by the General Council of the TUC as a trade union. If the union is affiliated to the Labour Party, individual party members must contribute to its political fund. Women's sections and branches of the Labour Party Young Socialists provide additional facilities for women members and for young members up to 25 years of age.

The CLPs administer their own affairs, elect their own officers, raise and administer their own funds, undertake their own publicity programmes, select their candidates and appoint their agents subject to the approval of the national organisation, and conduct election campaigns in the constituency on behalf of the Party.

The affairs of the CLPs are controlled by a general committee, which consists of delegates elected by the affiliated organisations and branches of individual members. An executive committee is elected annually by the general committee from among its own members to direct the work of the association under its supervision. The executive committee normally consists of the officers of the CLP (the president or chairman, two vice-presidents, treasurer and secretary) and as many additional members as the general committee thinks appropriate. The executive committee may set up sub-committees to deal with the social and recreational aspects of the work of the CLP, with the distribution of publicity material and with the usual range of political activity.

Liberal Party

Liberal constituency associations are similar to those of the Conservative Party in that they are composed of individual members, who acquire membership through annual subscriptions to the local party funds. They are responsible for their own organisation, working arrangements and finance; they sponsor Liberal candidates in local and national elections; and they are expected to keep watch upon the legislative and administrative work of the Government, especially as it affects the needs and interests of the district, and to direct the attention of local authorities, the public and the Press to the importance of these subjects, and to the methods by which Liberals believe they should be handled. There are also local branches of the Young Liberals and the Women's Liberal Federation.

Social Democratic Party

The basic unit of organisation in the country is the area party, usually consisting of more than one parliamentary constituency. To date there are some 200 area parties covering every constituency in England, Wales and Scotland. Membership is open to anyone over the age of 16 who supports the aims outlined in the Party's membership leaflet.

Constituency Agents

In each constituency, an agent is appointed by each party as the chief organiser of party activities in the area. Some of these agents are full-time salaried officials, who hold certificates (issued by the party headquarters) which guarantee their knowledge of election law and allied matters, although there are also many part-time or voluntary agents, particularly in the Labour and Liberal parties. About 50 per cent of Conservative constituency associations have a paid full-time, part-time or shared agent, compared with about 15 per cent of the Labour constituency parties and 10 per cent of the Liberal associations. The duties of the agent include acting as secretary to the constituency association and serving as executive assistant to the local MP. Before elections, the agent is also expected to act as business manager to the prospective candidate and to ensure that election campaigns are conducted within the law. In constituencies where there is no full-time agent, part-time or voluntary election agents or organisers may be appointed. The salaries of most agents are borne on constituency association funds, but the Labour Party head office contributes towards the cost of some 26 agents in key constituencies.

Parliamentary Candidates

Prospective candidates are chosen by the constituency associations of each party according to their own established practice. Sitting MPs in all parties are required to be readopted by their constituency associations at some point before contesting a general election.

Procedure in the *Conservative Party* is as follows: when a new candidate is to be chosen, the executive council of the constituency association appoints a selection committee to which the Standing Advisory Committee on Candidates at party headquarters submits a list of potential candidates who have indicated their wish to stand for that constituency. The names of local party members, some of whom may have put forward their own names for consideration, are also submitted. When any new local names have been approved by the standing committee, the selection committee chooses a number of candidates for interview, and produces a short list to appear before the whole executive council. A series of ballots is then taken, as a result of which one candidate is recommended to a general meeting of the whole constituency association. Except on the rarest occasions, this candidate is formally adopted. During the past ten years or so an increasing number of constituency associations have presented a choice of two or three potential candidates chosen by the executive council to a general meeting, rather than just one recommended candidate.

In the *Labour Party*, when a decision has been made (in consultation with the national organisation) to contest an election and a new candidate is to be chosen, affiliated and party organisations within the constituency are invited to nominate a candidate. A nomination may also be made by the executive committee of the constituency association and, in by-elections only, by the National Executive Committee (NEC); but individuals may not submit their own names. The executive committee of the Constituency Labour Party then examines all nominations and proposes a short list to go before the general committee, which has power to amend it. This is followed by a selection conference composed of the delegates of the general committee. At this meeting, which is usually attended by a representative from the Party's regional office, a vote is taken by successive ballots, until one prospective candidate has obtained a clear majority of the total votes cast. The name of the selected candidate is then placed before a meeting of the NEC for endorsement.

Under new rules introduced in 1980, the Labour Party has adopted the compulsory mid-term reselection of parliamentary candidates, including MPs. The final choice is made by the constituency general management committee sitting in its special capacity as a 'selection conference'. This provides a formal opportunity for reselection or replacement.

Liberal Party procedure involves setting up a selection committee to produce a short list for submission to a general meeting of a Liberal association. Normally this will contain at least three names drawn from the list of approved candidates from among which the association will choose by secret ballot using the alternative vote system of proportional representation. The executive may, however, decide to propose to the general meeting the readoption, without competition, of the candidate at the last election.

In the *Social Democratic Party* members interested in standing for Parliament must first apply for inclusion on the Party's approved list of candidates. The area party committee draws up a short list which must include two women, and then calls a general meeting where members may question the applicants. The actual selection is decided by a postal ballot of the area party members using the single transferable vote system.

Regional Organisation

The constituency associations of the Conservative, Labour and Liberal parties are grouped into regional organisations which focus party political opinion over a wide region and are thus able to provide co-ordinated advice and information for the central organisation and party leaders.

The Conservative Party has 11 'provincial' areas in England and Wales, each having an area council on which all the constituencies in the area are represented. Scotland is split into three areas, each with an area council to which six representatives are sent by each constituency in the region.

The Labour Party has 11 regional councils whose membership is open to: constituency parties affiliated to the Labour Party at national level; county (regional in

Scotland) Labour parties; trade unions affiliated to the Labour Party and the Trades Union Congress at national level; district councils of nationally affiliated trade unions; co-operative societies or organisations; socialist societies affiliated to the Labour Party nationally; women's councils; and federations of trades councils. There are also district Labour parties corresponding to the areas of local government district councils. Both Wales and Scotland have a Labour Party regional council.

There are 13 regional Liberal organisations in England and independent Liberal parties in Wales and Scotland.

National Organisation

Conservative Party

The central pillar of the party organisation in England and Wales is the National Union of Conservative and Unionist[1] Associations, a federal organisation to which are affiliated some 550 constituency associations. Scotland has its own organisation, the Scottish Conservative and Unionist Association, but its 72 constituency associations are now also affiliated to the National Union. The main function of the National Union is to advance the Party's cause and to serve as a deliberative and advisory body which keeps the leader informed of party opinion.

The governing body of the National Union is the Central Council, which meets once a year to debate motions which have been submitted from constituencies, areas and national advisory committees, and to elect the officers of the National Union. Membership includes the leader of the Party and other principal officers and officials; the Conservative members of both Houses of Parliament and of the European Parliament; the members of the Executive Committee; and six adopted representatives from each constituency association, together with representatives from the Scottish Association, provincial area councils and national committees.

The Executive Committee of the National Union (which meets regularly) is composed of 200 members, including representatives of the provincial area councils (who, in turn, represent the constituencies in the areas) and the leader and other principal officers of the Party. The Committee has authority to perform all ordinary and emergency acts on behalf of the Central Council in the intervals between the latter's meetings. Its special functions include: recommending to the Central Council for election the officers of the National Union; approving the admission of constituency associations to the National Union; settling disputes between or within constituency associations; considering resolutions or reports on party or public affairs submitted by the provincial areas or constituencies and forwarding them to the appropriate quarters; electing representatives of the National Union to the various national committees of the Party; and submitting an annual report to the party conference. The Executive Committee is advised by National Advisory Committees: the Conservative Women's National Committee; the Young Conservative National Advisory Committee; the Conservative Trade Unionists' National Committee; the National Local Government Advisory

---

[1] *The word 'Unionist' in the title stems from the amalgamation in 1912 of the Conservative Party and the Liberal Unionists who had broken away from the rest of the Liberal Party in 1886 over a dispute concerning Home Rule for Ireland, in which they favoured a continuation of the union with that country.*

Committee; the National Advisory Committee on Education; the Conservative Political Centre National Advisory Committee; and the Federation of Conservative Students.

There are also a number of other central committees or boards, some of which report to the Executive Committee, and they occupy an important place in party organisation. They are: the Advisory Committee on Policy, which is responsible solely to the party leader; the Conservative Party Board of Finance; the Standing Advisory Committees on United Kingdom and European Candidates; the Examination Board (for agents and organisers); and the Superannuation Fund.

An annual conference, lasting four days, is held by the National Union every year and is the most important annual gathering of the Party. The conference is attended by the members of the Central Council and two additional representatives of each constituency—one of whom must be a Young Conservative—including certificated agents or organisers. At this the National Union receives the report of the Executive Committee, and debates and passes resolutions on party policy. It is not authorised to formulate policy and has no executive power; its resolutions are therefore not binding on the party leadership, but they have considerable influence. Annual conferences are also held by the Party in Scotland and Wales.

Labour Party

The highest authority in the Labour Party is the party conference, which directs and controls the work of the Party outside Parliament, frames and amends its constitution and standing orders, and formulates, in broad outline, the party policy. The conference is normally held once a year for four and a half days and is attended by some 1,100 delegates appointed by trade unions, constituency parties and socialist and co-operative societies. *Ex officio* members such as leading officials of the Party, MPs and prospective parliamentary candidates, and constituency party agents take part.

Seven-eighths of the votes at the conference are held by the trade unions, distributed in proportion to the money that each union pays annually as an affiliation fee; the payment is made from union members' contributions to political funds.

The National Executive Committee (NEC) is the administrative authority of the Party and seeks to apply its policies between annual party conferences. It consists of 29 members, two of whom are *ex officio*—the leader and the deputy leader of the Party. The treasurer and 25 members are elected every year at the annual conference, on the following basis: 12 members by the trade union delegates; 7 by the constituency party delegates; 1 by the delegates of socialist, co-operative and professional organisations; and 5 women members elected by the conference as a whole (as is the treasurer). The Labour Party Young Socialists also have a representative who is elected by their annual conference. The NEC elects its own chairman and vice-chairman every year. Its functions are to supervise the work of the Party outside Parliament at every level, and to report on its own work to the conference, submitting to it 'such resolutions and declarations affecting the programme, principles and policy of the Party as, in its view, may be necessitated by political circumstances'.

The NEC works through a number of committees (Organisation, International, Home Policy, Press and Publicity, Youth, and Finance and General Purposes), two of which (the International and Home Policy committees) have a number of special sub-committees and working parties appointed to deal with particular areas of policy or problems of current concern to the Party. The leader of the Party, the   13 deputy leader, and the chairman, vice-chairman and the treasurer of the NEC are *ex officio* members of each committee; the remaining members are elected through the NEC itself.

The NEC also participates in a number of general committees with other representative Labour organisations. The most important of these is the National Council of Labour, which is composed of seven representatives of the Trades Union Congress, seven representatives of the Co-operative Union,[1] and seven representatives of the Labour Party. The NEC does not maintain a formal link with the Fabian Society, but there are close ties between them; each month the society publishes pamphlets on social, economic, political and international issues, many of which aim to influence the formation of Labour Party policy. There is also a National Women's Advisory Committee, which advises the NEC on questions concerning the organisation and work of women in the Party.

Liberal Party

The Liberal Party determines the broad outlines of party policy through its annual conference, known as the Joint Assembly, which is attended by representatives of all constituency associations and recognised units, together with certain *ex officio* members, such as MPs, candidates and agents. In addition to electing the president, party treasurer and some members of the Party Council, the Assembly receives reports on the work of the Party and debates policy resolutions proposed by the constituency associations or other organs of the Party, and resolutions from commissions which meet at the start of the Assembly.

The Party Council, with 275 members, meets quarterly in different parts of the country; it includes 30 representatives of the Party in both Houses of Parliament, and members elected by the regional federations, the Women Liberals, the Young Liberals and others. Its chief duty is 'to stimulate militant Liberalism in every part of the country' and 'to express the views of the Liberal Party on current political issues'. Resolutions on aspects of party policy are debated and, if passed by both the Assembly and the Council, become official party policy.

Between meetings of the Council, the day-to-day work of the Party is directed by the National Executive Committee (NEC) which consists of 50 to 60 members. It meets about eight times a year and the party chairman presides. A Finance and Administration Board is responsible for fund-raising, control of finance and administering the party headquarters. A standing committee, chaired by an MP appointed by the parliamentary party and meeting once a month, is responsible for developing party policy and the specialist advisory panels.

The Scottish and Welsh Liberal parties are independent constituent parties of the federal Liberal Party of the United Kingdom. They have separate organisations, hold annual conferences and each has its own Party Council and Executive.

Social Democratic Party

Responsibility for the Party's affairs outside Parliament is handled by an elected National Committee. This consists of 38 members and meets at least once a month (except

---

[1] *Representing the interests of the Co-operative movement.*

August) under the chairmanship of the party president. A Policy Sub-Committee is responsible for preparing the Party's election programme, based on policy statements adopted by the Council for Social Democracy. This Council, which is responsible for deciding party policy, meets at least three times a year and consists of a president, all SDP MPs, members co-opted by the Council, and representatives from the area parties.

A Consultative Assembly is held at least once a year to provide a forum for party members to discuss the policy and programme of the Party and the conduct of its affairs. The Assembly is chaired by the president, and all party members are entitled to apply for tickets to attend. The choice of issues to be debated at the Assembly rests with the Assembly Committee, subject to the direction of the National Committee.

Central Offices

Each main party has a national headquarters, staffed by full-time professional workers who co-ordinate party organisation and prepare various party publications, including general outlines of policy and pamphlets on particular topics.

The *Conservative* Central Office, along with its 11 area offices, is presided over by a chairman, assisted by one deputy chairman and four vice-chairmen of the party organisation and two treasurers. Three vice-chairmen are responsible respectively for parliamentary candidature, local government and the women's organisation. The executive vice-chairman is responsible for the day-to-day management of Central Office, for financial control and for co-ordinating the detailed development of election preparations. All these appointments are made by the leader of the Party.

Central Office departments include those dealing with organisation and community affairs, marketing, publicity, speakers, finance, training, trade unions, local government, women, the Young Conservatives, ethnic minority groups, European Parliament elections, the Federation of Students, and small businesses. The marketing and publicity departments are responsible for developing communication techniques both inside and outside the Party.

Two additional organisations of great importance, both of them forming part of Central Office, are the Conservative Research Department and the Conservative Political Centre. The Conservative Research Department, which is responsible to the party leader through the party chairman, plays an important part in developing party policies. On a day-to-day basis, the Research Department is responsible for briefing the parliamentary party (including the Cabinet when the Conservative Party is in power) and servicing Conservative back-bench committees. It draws up policy proposals for Cabinet consideration, provides factual material for party publicity and itself produces reference works. It has four major sections: economic, home affairs, political and constitutional, and the International Office. The International Office provides briefing on aspects of foreign policy, carries out research into international affairs, assists liaison between the European Parliament and Westminster, and acts as the point of first contact with the Party for organisations and individuals from other countries, foreign journalists and diplomatic missions. The Conservative Political Centre provides political education facilities for party members and others interested in politics, through constituency discussion groups, seminars, weekend schools, and publications by MPs and others.

The headquarters of the *Labour Party* is composed of six departments: General Secretary's Department, National Agent's Department, the International Department,

Research Department, the Press and Publicity Department and the Finance Department. The chief official is the General Secretary, who works immediately under the direction of the NEC, and is elected by the annual conference on the recommendation of the NEC. The other leading officials are the National Agent, with two Assistant National Agents (one responsible for women's activities and one for youth), and the heads of departments.

The staff of the General Secretary's Department serve as executive assistants to the General Secretary and are therefore concerned with the entire work of the Party. The International Department is responsible for maintaining contacts with socialist parties in foreign countries and in the Commonwealth.[1] All the departments are responsible to committees of the NEC, except the General Secretary's Department, which reports directly to the NEC itself.

The headquarters of the *Liberal Party* is responsible to the Finance and Administration Board, which consists of the party treasurer, the head of the Liberal Party Organisation, four members elected by the NEC and two elected by the staff association of the Liberal Party headquarters. It provides secretarial and executive assistance to all the national organs of the Party and their committees, and support for parliamentary candidates, and is also responsible for publicity, organisation, information and research. The Chief Whip (see p 20) is responsible for the employment of support staff and research assistants for the parliamentary party: these are funded partly by government grant (see p 22).

The headquarters of the *Social Democratic Party* comprises the Office of the Chief Executive and the departments of the National Secretary, National Organiser, Director of Communications, and Policy Co-ordinator. It is staffed by a small team of paid officials, supported by a number of volunteers.

Party Finance

The main parties derive their funds from various sources. The central income of the Conservative Party comes from voluntary subscriptions consisting of individual as well as company contributions, with the addition of contributions from the constituency associations assessed on an agreed basis. There is no fixed subscription. Almost 90 per cent of the income of the Labour Party is provided by annual affiliation fees of 45 pence per member payable by trade unions; the remainder is provided by the constituency associations on the basis of individual membership, each individual member paying a minimum subscription of £6, with reduced rates for the elderly and the unemployed, and from socialist societies and one large co-operative society.

The Liberal Party's funds consist of individual donations, an annual affiliation fee from constituency associations, contributions from constituency associations assessed under a combined finance scheme, financial appeals and a variety of fund-raising schemes. The minimum subscription fee for members is £5.

Social Democratic Party funds consist of subscriptions and contributions from individual members and supporters. There is no fixed subscription, but a minimum requirement of £4.

In 1977–78 (the latest date for which figures are available), the Conservative Party received a central income of approximately £2·7 million. In 1981 the Labour Party's

---

[1] *The Labour Party is a member of the Socialist International, which consists of nearly 40 labour, socialist and social democratic parties in various countries throughout the world.*

central income was just over £3·2 million. The central income of the Liberal Party headquarters in London in 1981 was almost £200,000, with the Scottish and Welsh Liberal parties receiving £50,000 and £10,000 respectively. The income of the Social Democratic Party in its first year of existence was about £750,000.

No political party is legally obliged to publish its accounts; however, business firms required to publish their accounts under company law must show the amounts of contributions above £50 made to political party funds.

The Party Leaders

The powers of the party leaders and the method of their appointment differ among the parties. However, in all cases, if a party wins a general election, it is the leader who is called upon by the Sovereign to form a government, as Prime Minister, and who is then entitled to choose the members of the administration.

In the Conservative Party, the party leader is elected by Conservative MPs in a secret ballot. In the Labour Party, the leader's appointment is decided on a broader basis—by election by representatives of the affiliated trade unions, the constituency parties, and the parliamentary party. The Liberal Party leader is elected by party members throughout Britain. Both the leader and the president of the SDP are elected by a postal ballot of the national membership.

Once elected, the leaders of the Conservative, Labour and Liberal parties become the national leaders of their parties inside and outside Parliament.

The leader of the Conservative Party is the Prime Minister, Mrs Margaret Thatcher, MP (elected in 1975), while the leader of the Labour Party is Mr Michael Foot, MP (elected in 1980). Mr David Steel, MP, has been leader of the Liberal Party since 1976, and Mr Roy Jenkins, MP, was elected leader of the SDP in 1982.

Conservative Party

When the Conservative Party is in opposition, the leader is subject to annual re-election normally on the opening of a new parliamentary session, or within six months of a general election. When the party forms the Government, the leader is normally re-elected automatically. The Conservative leader is elected by Conservative MPs, who nominate candidates.

If necessary there are three ballots. A candidate is elected on the first ballot if he or she receives both an overall majority of votes and 15 per cent more votes than any other candidate. Before the ballot an opportunity is provided for Conservative constituency associations to make their views known. If no winner emerges on the first ballot, a second one is held and nominations for the first are void. Candidates who did not stand in the first ballot may stand in the second. The winner of the second ballot is the candidate receiving more than 50 per cent of votes. A third ballot is organised if there is no second ballot winner. The three candidates receiving the highest number of votes at the second ballot go forward to the final ballot where voters indicate their first and second choices. The candidate with the lowest number of first preferences is eliminated and the votes of those giving him or her as their first preference are redistributed among the other two in accordance with their second preferences.

Once the result of the election has been declared, the winner is presented for confirmation as leader of the Conservative Party to a meeting of Conservative MPs and peers, adopted parliamentary candidates and members of the Executive Committee of the National Union of Conservative and Unionist Associations.

The Conservative Party leader is responsible for the formulation of party policy. Although kept constantly aware through the various party organisations of the feelings and opinions of Conservative supporters throughout the country, the party leader is not normally required to report on his or her work either inside or outside Parliament. The Conservative leader attends several sessions of the Party's annual conference and addresses the representatives.

When Leader of the Opposition the Conservative leader chooses a 'shadow cabinet' of about 18 MPs and peers to serve as a consultative committee and, at all times, is in complete charge of the party headquarters, with the right to appoint all its officers. The powers of the Conservative leader are exercised only with the consent of the Party; if there is clear evidence that this consent is being withdrawn, the leader has no alternative but to resign.

Labour Party

The leader of the Labour Party, like that of the Conservative Party, is subject when in opposition to annual re-election. When the Party is in office, elections for the leadership take place only when a vacancy occurs through the death or resignation of the Prime Minister.

Candidates for election to the Labour Party leadership must be MPs and, under new rules approved in 1981 which widen the franchise for electing the leader, must be nominated by an electoral college- consisting of representatives from the affiliated trade unions, the constituency parties and the House of Commons members of the parliamentary party in ratios of 40:30:30 respectively. The successful candidate is the one who receives an overall majority of the votes cast, and successive ballots are held until this occurs. If after the first ballot no candidate has an overall majority, the candidate with the lowest vote drops out (or the two or three lowest-placed candidates if their combined votes amount to fewer than those of the candidates above them). After the first ballot, other candidates may also withdraw if they wish, but no new candidate may be nominated. The deputy leader of the Party is elected annually in the same manner.

The function of the Labour Party leader is to implement, as far as possible, the programme determined jointly by the Parliamentary Labour Party and the mass party organisations; and he attends the annual party conference to report on the work done in Parliament during the previous year. When he is Leader of the Opposition, he works with a 'shadow cabinet' (the Parliamentary Committee, see p 21) whose members are chosen by the Parliamentary Labour Party; the leader appoints the official spokesmen from the members of the elected Parliamentary Committee and other members of the Parliamentary Labour Party. He and his deputy are *ex officio* members of the National Executive Committee, which directs the operations of the party headquarters, but he is not in personal control.

Liberal Party

An election to the Liberal leadership takes place if the leader dies, resigns, or loses his seat in the House of Commons; if a majority of Liberal MPs pass a vote of no confidence in him; or if the leader asks for an election. An election may also be held if at least 50

Liberal constituency associations in at least eight of the national or regional areas petition for one.

Candidates for the Liberal leadership must be Liberal members of the House of Commons, nominated by five Liberal MPs, or one-fifth of Liberal members, whichever is the smaller. The leader of the Liberal Party is elected by paid-up members of the Party in the country, under a one-person, one-vote system.

Social Democratic Party

The Social Democratic Party has adopted a system of dual leadership: this consists of a leader who heads the parliamentary party and a president who oversees all non-parliamentary business and leads the Party outside the House of Commons. Both the leader and the president are elected by a postal ballot of all paid-up members of the Party. Candidates for the leadership must be SDP members of the House of Commons, nominated by not less than 15 per cent of the Party's MPs. Candidates for the office of president must be members of the Council for Social Democracy at the date of nomination and be nominated by at least 10 per cent of the members of the Council.

Party Organisation Inside Parliament

The Whips

In Parliament the parties are organised under officers known as 'Whips'.[1] The term applies to a member of a particular party in Parliament who is responsible for ensuring that MPs support their party in divisions (the taking of votes); it also applies to the weekly circular letter sent out by each Chief Whip to all MPs within a party requesting their attendance at appropriate times and notifying them of parliamentary business.[2]

The party whips consist of the Chief Whip and, in the two main parties, the Deputy Chief Whip and a varying number of junior whips, all of whom are MPs. Those of the party in power are known as Government Whips and are paid out of public funds.

There are Government and Opposition Whips in both Houses of Parliament, but the whips in the House of Lords are less exclusively concerned with party matters and, unlike those in the Commons, act as government spokesmen.

The Government Chief Whip is directly answerable to the Prime Minister and the Leader of the House of Commons. Subject to the Cabinet, the overriding responsibility for the organisation of business in the House of Commons and the progress of the Government's legislative programme rests with the Leader of the House. Under the authority of the Leader, the Government Chief Whip in the Commons attends the Cabinet and makes the day-to-day arrangements for the Government's programme of business (estimating the time likely to be required for each item and discussing the proposed business arrangements with the Opposition). The Chief Whip also has responsibilities for securing majorities for the Government. He is assisted by a very small Civil Service staff, headed by the Private Secretary, who is frequently consulted by the Leader of the House. The Opposition Chief Whip carries out equally responsible duties for his own party, and also receives a special salary. Two other Opposition Whips in the House of Commons also receive official salaries.

The Government and Opposition Chief Whips, who hold frequent consultations, together constitute the 'usual channels' often referred to in the House of Commons when the question of finding time for debating some particular issue or other parliamentary arrangements are discussed.

The Opposition Chief Whip receives advance notice of the Government's programme each week, and no final decision is taken until after conversations between him and the Government Chief Whip. The junior whips are responsible for keeping in touch with individual MPs and conveying their opinions to the Chief Whip. There are about 12 whips on each side, each responsible for 20 to 30 MPs, usually grouped on a regional basis.

In the House of Lords both the Government Chief Whip and the Opposition Chief

---

[1] *The term 'whip' derives from fox-hunting, where whippers-in or whips are used by a hunt to look after the hounds and prevent them from straying.*

[2] *The relative importance of attendance for debates and divisions listed in the circular notice is indicated by their being underlined once, twice or three times. Items underlined once are considered purely routine and attendance is optional; those underlined twice are more important and attendance is required unless a 'pair' (that is, a member of an opposition party who also intends to be absent from a division) has been arranged; items underlined three times are highly important and pairing is not normally allowed. Failure to attend after receiving a 'three-line Whip' renders a member liable to disciplinary action by his party.*

Whip receive a salary from public funds. The Government Chief Whip is assisted by Government Whips who, as in the House of Commons, are paid; the Opposition Whips are not paid.

Party Organisation

The most important organ of the Conservative Party in Parliament is the Conservative and Unionist Members' Committee, popularly known as the 1922 Committee. This Committee, named after the year in which it was formed, normally meets once a week and is composed of the entire back-bench membership of the Conservative Party. Although it is not authorised to formulate policy or to control, in any way directly, the activities of the Party's leader or front bench, it serves as a sounding board of Conservative opinion in the House of Commons, and it is upon this Committee's support that the leader's position in the Party depends. The Committee is autonomous and independent; it has its own organisation and its own members and, when there is a Conservative government, ministers attend its meetings by invitation and not by right; but when the Conservatives are in opposition, the whole membership of the Party is eligible to attend meetings. The Committee is presided over by a chairman (elected annually), two vice-chairmen, two secretaries and a treasurer, who, together with 12 others elected by the Committee from among its members, constitute an executive committee, which meets weekly, immediately before the meeting of the full Committee. Major issues of party or government policy are discussed at meetings of the 1922 Committee, but votes are not normally taken, the chairman being expected to interpret 'the sense of the meeting'. There are no members of the House of Lords in the 1922 Committee: Conservative peers hold their meetings separately. When the Party is in opposition, the leader appoints the consultative committee which acts as the Party's 'shadow cabinet' and which is separate from the executive committee of the 1922 Committee.

The Parliamentary Labour Party (PLP) is composed of all Labour members in both Houses. When the Labour Party is in office, a liaison committee acts as a channel of communication between the Government and its back-benchers in both Houses. Half of the committee is elected by the back-bench Labour members of the House of Commons and the remainder are representatives of the Government; these include the Leader of the House, the Government Chief Whip and four others, including a Labour peer, appointed by the party leader. When Labour is in opposition, the PLP is organised under the direction of the Parliamentary Committee (often referred to as the 'shadow cabinet') consisting of six *ex officio* members: the leader of the party, the deputy leader, the chairman of the parliamentary party, the Labour Chief Whips from both Houses of Parliament, and the Leader of the Labour peers; 12 elected representatives of Labour MPs; and one elected representative of the Labour peers.

Meetings of the PLP, at which broad outlines of policy are discussed and important decisions sometimes taken, are held regularly each week and may be convened more often. The party leader and his colleagues are eligible to attend and do so whenever possible, whether the Party is in or out of office. In general, the PLP has a greater measure of influence in the formulation of policy than has its Conservative counterpart.

The Liberal Party meets each week to discuss forthcoming parliamentary business and other matters, the leader taking the chair. All MPs and several peers attend.

All Social Democratic Party MPs belong to the Parliamentary Committee which conducts the Party's activities in the House of Commons. The Committee also includes representatives of the SDP members of the House of Lords. Although they must have full regard to the adopted policies of the SDP, the MPs are not subject to direction by the Party.

Representatives from both the Liberal and Social Democratic parties meet each week to co-ordinate views on parliamentary issues.

Party Committees

In addition to their membership of the party meetings, both Conservative and Labour MPs have a policy committee system, organised around subject areas roughly corresponding to those of government departments, although not necessarily covering them all. Both main parties have about 20 groups of this kind, including, for instance, agriculture and food, economic affairs and finance, trade and industry, education, science and technology, aviation, foreign and Commonwealth affairs, and overseas development. In the Parliamentary Labour Party there are also regional groups. The Liberal Party has policy panels reporting to a standing committee which advises Liberal MPs and develops party policy. Membership is voluntary.

Financial Assistance to Opposition Parties

Provision is made for financial assistance from public funds to opposition parties to help them carry out their parliamentary work at Westminster. The amounts provided are based on a formula related to votes received and seats won at the previous general election.

Assistance is limited to those parties which had at least two members elected at the previous general election, or which had one member elected and received a minimum of 150,000 votes. The amount given is £962·50 for every seat and £1·9 for every 200 votes, with an upper limit of £290,000. Since the Conservative Party is at present the governing party, the amounts given between 1979 and 1981 to parties were as follows: Labour Party £512,198; Liberal Party £86,737; Scottish National Party £11,282; Plaid Cymru (Welsh Nationalist) £2,126; Official Unionist Party £12,084; Democratic Unionist Party £5,940. Parties are accountable for expenditure to the Accounting Officer of the House of Commons. The allocation of a party's entitlement between its work in the House of Commons and the House of Lords is decided by the party itself.

The Nationalist Parties: Scottish National Party and Plaid Cymru

The Scottish National Party (SNP) and Plaid Cymru (Welsh Nationalist) each returned two members to Parliament in the 1979 general election. The SNP received 504,259 votes or 17·3 per cent of the total vote in Scotland; Plaid Cymru received 132,544 votes or 8·1 per cent of the total vote in Wales.

The organisation of the two parties, which has many features in common, is outlined below.

Branches and Constituency Associations

The basic unit of organisation in both the Scottish National Party and Plaid Cymru is the branch, rather than the constituency association. This is partly due to the large geographical area of many constituencies in the rural regions of Scotland and Wales, which makes the organisation of the parties more convenient at a more local level. Delegates from the branches of both parties are appointed to the constituency associations. Both the SNP and Plaid Cymru consist of individual members who pay an annual membership fee; the SNP also has three affiliated organisations. In both parties parliamentary candidates are chosen by the constituency associations in consultation with their respective National Executive Committees.

National Organisation

The annual conference of the SNP is its 'supreme governing body'. The National Council, which meets quarterly, is the Party's governing body between conferences. Delegates to the annual conference and National Council are appointed by and from the branches and constituency associations. Two affiliated organisations—the Federation of Student Nationalists and Young Scottish Nationalists (a youth organisation)—are also represented.

The annual conference of Plaid Cymru is likewise the supreme authority within the Party. Between conferences, which are attended by delegates from the branches, the National Council assumes responsibility for taking tactical policy decisions. It comprises two representatives from each constituency, together with prospective parliamentary candidates and national officials. Management and finance decisions are taken by the Party's National Executive Committee which meets monthly and comprises elected national officers and representatives of the county organisations.

Central Offices

The headquarters of the SNP comprises four departments: organisation and administration, public relations, research, and publications. Plaid Cymru has a national office with a general secretary and executive secretary dealing with public relations, election organisation, finance and internal administration.

Party Finance

About two-thirds of the SNP's central income is derived from membership subscriptions; the Party does not publish an annual income figure. Three-quarters of Plaid Cymru's   23 total income comes from donations other than those from the constituency parties, and from miscellaneous sources, including the sale of literature. The Party's income in 1981 was an estimated £85,000.

Party Leaders

In the SNP the offices of leader of the Party at large and leader of the MPs in the House of Commons are separate. The leader of the SNP members in the House of Commons is responsible for the day-to-day tactics of the Party in Parliament, within the broad policy framework agreed by the Party's annual conference. The leader of the Party outside the Commons, however, is the chairman, who is elected (or re-elected) annually by the party conference. He is responsible for the Party's overall organisation. The leader of the SNP in the House of Commons is Mr Donald Stewart, MP, who was elected in 1974, and the chairman of the Party is Mr Gordon Wilson, MP, elected in 1979.

The leader of Plaid Cymru, known as the president, need not necessarily be an MP. He has traditionally been chosen directly by the party conference every two years, but, as a result of constitutional changes passed in 1981, future elections of the president and senior vice-president will take place by ballot held in party branches and area meetings. The election is for a two-year term. The president of Plaid Cymru is Mr Dafydd Wigley, MP, elected in 1981.

Northern Ireland Parties

Members from Northern Ireland constituencies belong to political parties organised separately from those in Great Britain.

Northern Ireland representation at Westminster was dominated for over 50 years by the Ulster Unionist Party, whose origins lie in the Ulster Unionist Council, a coalition formed in 1906 by various unionist groups opposed to the Home Rule movement for Ireland. The Council still controls the machinery and policy of the Party, now referred to as the Official Unionist Party. Changes in policy introduced in the 1960s produced divisions within the Unionist Party and led to the formation of the Protestant Unionist Party which emerged from a group known as Ulster Protestant Action. In 1971 this Party changed its name to the Democratic Unionist Party.

The Social Democratic and Labour Party, which is non-sectarian but largely Roman Catholic in support, was founded in 1970 from a combination of former nationalist and Republican groups. The Alliance Party was founded in 1970 on non-sectarian principles.

At the general election in May 1979 the 12 Northern Ireland seats were distributed as follows: Official Unionist 5; Democratic Unionist 3; United Ulster Unionist 1; Ulster Unionist 1; Social Democratic and Labour 1; Independent 1. As a result of subsequent resignations, the Social Democratic and Labour MP, Mr Gerard Fitt (who was the leader of the Party), now sits as Socialist, and the Ulster Unionist MP, Mr James Kilfedder, sits as Ulster Popular Unionist. After the death of the Independent member (for Fermanagh and South Tyrone) in March 1981 the seat was held for a short time by Mr Robert Sands, a Republican prisoner in Maze Prison, who was elected as an anti-H-Block supporter. Following Mr Sands's death in May 1981, the seat was won by Mr Owen Carron, also an anti-H-Block supporter.

The total number of votes gained by the four main political parties in Northern Ireland and their percentage of the total vote in the Province in the 1979 general election were as follows:

Party	Total votes	Percentage of total vote
Official Unionist (OUP)	254,578	36·6
Democratic Unionist (DUP)	70,975	10·2
Social Democratic and Labour (SDLP)	137,110	19·7
Alliance	82,892	11·9

In the elections to the Northern Ireland Assembly[1] which took place on 20 October 1982, using the single transferable vote system of proportional representation, the 78 seats (with first-preference percentages) were distributed as shown in the table on p 26.

The organisation of the four main parties is given on p 26.

Branches and Constituency Associations

Outside Parliament, the basic units of organisation in the *Official Unionist Party*,

---

[1] *The Assembly, which held its first meeting on 11 November 1982, is to recommend arrangements for the partial or full devolution of powers to Northern Ireland.*

	Percentage of first-preference votes	Seats
OUP	29·8	26
DUP	23·0	21
SDLP	18·8	14
Alliance	9·3	10
Sinn Fein*	10·2	5
Others	9·0	2†

* The political wing of the Provisional Irish Republican Army.

† Two seats were won by independent Unionists, one of whom, James Kilfedder, MP, the leader of the Ulster Popular Unionist Party, has since been elected Presiding Officer.

which itself has recently been restructured to take account of the proposed increase from 12 to 17 parliamentary constituencies,[1] are the local branches which are based mainly on local government electoral wards. A number of branches together form the local constituency association which is responsible for electing its own officers, and delegates to the Council and party executive, as well as selecting candidates for parliamentary and other elections.

In the *Democratic Unionist Party* membership of the local branch is open to anyone aged 18 years or over who is on the electoral register for the area covered by the branch and who has given a written undertaking to subscribe to the constitution and rules of the Party. Each branch elects its own officers annually and is allowed to formulate whatever rules it considers necessary, providing these do not conflict with the party constitution and rules. All branches within a constituency are affiliated to the local constituency association which meets at least three times a year. Full members elect annually the leading officers of the association and whatever other officers they think appropriate. They also elect four members to represent the constituency on the Central Executive Committee (see p 28). Each association has a standing committee with overall responsibility for organising and co-ordinating its affairs, subject to the approval of the full association. It includes two representatives elected each year from every local branch within the constituency.

In the *Social Democratic and Labour Party* branches have two classes of membership: individual members and corporate members. Individual members must be attached to the appropriate branch operating in the constituency where they live or where they are registered as electors, and must subscribe to the principles and objectives of the Party. Corporate members consist of trade unions affiliated to the Irish Congress of Trade Unions, co-operative societies, socialist societies, professional associations and cultural organisations. Branches appoint delegates to the local constituency council whose functions are to promote the policies of the Party; co-ordinate the work of the constituency branches; and create and maintain an effective electoral organisation within the constituency. Both branches and constituency councils elect their leading officers at an annual general meeting.

The basic organising unit of the *Alliance Party* is the constituency association, whose territorial boundary corresponds to the district council, except in Belfast where, instead of a single association, there are eight associations covering each electoral

---

[1] *The House of Commons (Redistribution of Seats) Act 1979 provides for the number of parliamentary constituencies in Northern Ireland to be increased from 12 to 17.*

district in the city. All associations may form one or more branches based mainly on local government electoral wards. At an annual general meeting each association elects its officers, an executive committee, delegates to the party council and to the annual conference, as well as one delegate for every 1,000 parliamentary electors within that part of the constituency served by the association to form the constituency's United Kingdom Election Delegate Convention.

rliamentary Candidates

The selection of prospective parliamentary candidates for the *Official Unionist Party* begins with the placing of advertisements in the local press inviting applications; these are then normally processed by the local executive or management committee which may either draft a short list or place all applicants before a selection conference. Candidates are given the opportunity to address the selection meeting and to answer questions, and voting continues until one candidate obtains an overall majority.

In the *Democratic Unionist Party* prospective parliamentary candidates are selected by the constituency association, with voting taking place by secret ballot. The names of the selected candidates are submitted to the Central Executive Committee for final endorsement.

In the *Social Democratic and Labour Party* prospective parliamentary candidates are chosen by a selection convention consisting of delegates appointed by branches affiliated to the constituency council, and organised by the Executive Committee. A prospective candidate must be proposed and seconded in writing by individual party members, and the nomination forwarded to the Executive Committee. The candidate is elected by secret ballot, each delegate at the convention having one vote. The Executive Committee has the power to ratify or to refuse to ratify the choice of candidates.

Any member wishing to have his name placed on the *Alliance Party*'s list of approved parliamentary candidates must apply in writing to the general secretary of the Party, after which the application is considered by the candidate's sub-committee. The local delegate convention, which is convened and chaired by an election organiser (appointed by the Executive Committee), selects a candidate from the Party's approved list. Selection is by secret ballot using the alternative vote system, and the candidate with over 50 per cent of the votes is selected.

nnual Conferences, Executive Committees and Party Councils

The *Official Unionist Party* holds an annual conference organised by the Party's Central Executive Committee. Constituency associations and affiliated bodies are entitled to forward resolutions for consideration; these are then submitted to the executive committee which may approve, amend or reject them.

The Party Executive comprises four delegates from each constituency association and delegates from affiliated groups, the Women's Unionist Council, the Young Unionists and the Orange Order.[1]

The governing body of the Party is the Ulster Unionist Council which is responsible for the general organisation and promotion of the Party's affairs, including the annual election of party officers, among them the party leader. As with the Party Executive, the

---

[1] *The Loyal Orange Institution of Ireland, known as the Orange Order, was founded in its present form in 1795 as an exclusively Protestant body pledged to defend 'civil and religious liberty'.*

Council's officers are subject to annual election, and the general practice is that no one holds a particular office for more than two years.

The *Democratic Unionist Party* holds an annual conference which any party member may attend, but at which only delegates may vote. The conference is organised by the Central Executive Committee, and local branches and constituency associations are entitled to forward resolutions which are submitted to the Central Executive Committee for consideration.

The Central Executive Committee controls the day-to-day business of the Party and consists of members elected by and from each constituency association as well as the party leader and deputy leader. The leading officers of the Committee, who are also officers of the central delegates assembly, are elected annually by secret ballot from among its members.

The central delegates assembly, which ratifies all party manifestos, consists of members elected by and from each local branch as well as the members of the Central Executive Committee.

The supreme governing authority in the *Social Democratic and Labour Party* is the party conference which decides the Party's policies. It is normally held once a year and is attended by delegates appointed both by branches and by corporate members. Each delegate attending the conference has one vote. The conference elects the leading party officers, including the chairman and two vice-chairmen. Elections are by secret ballot using the single transferable vote system.

The Executive Committee is the administrative authority of the Party and controls its day-to-day organisation. It interprets the Party's constitution and is responsible for implementing conference decisions and developing policy between conferences. The Committee, which meets at least 12 times a year, consists of the party officers and 15 individual members elected at the conference.

There is also a Central Council whose function is to provide a means of communication between the membership and the central organisation of the Party. It meets twice a year and includes branch representatives and representatives from each constituency council and each district executive.

The *Alliance Party* holds an annual conference, organised by a conference committee appointed by the Executive Committee. Those entitled to attend include all party officers, members of the Executive Committee, elected public representatives of the Party and delegates from each constituency association and other affiliated groups. The conference elects the party president, who may hold office for not more than two consecutive years, and up to ten vice-presidents; it also considers policy resolutions proposed by the Executive Committee or by affiliated groups.

The Executive Committee carries out the day-to-day business of the Party, subject to the direction and control of the Party Council. The Committee, which meets at least once a month, consists of the party officers and 15 party members elected by the Council. It presents a progress report at each meeting and an annual report to conference on the work of the Party.

The Party Council is the supreme governing body of the Party and decides party policies. It has at least four meetings a year, one of which is the annual general meeting of the Party at which the Executive Committee is elected. The Council consists of the party officers, members of the Executive Committee and delegates from the constituency associations.

rty Leaders

Until 1972 *Official Unionist* MPs took the Conservative Whip at Westminster, and the formal connection between the parties still remains. However, since the suspension of the Stormont Parliament in 1972, Official Unionists have operated in Parliament as an independent force and sit on the Opposition benches. The leader of the Party is elected at the annual general meeting of the Council. Mr James Molyneaux, MP, has been the leader of the Official Unionist Party since 1979.

In the *Democratic Unionist Party* the objectives of the parliamentary party include providing a forum for consultation and action for the party's MPs, and co-ordinating the efforts and membership of the parliamentary party. It elects officers annually from among its membership and fills any other posts it considers necessary. The leader of the Democratic Unionist Party is the Reverend Ian Paisley, MP, elected in 1971.

The leader of the *Social Democratic and Labour Party* has traditionally been elected by the Party's parliamentary group following a general election; the method of election is at present under review. Mr John Hume has been leader of the Social Democratic and Labour Party since 1980.

In the *Alliance Party*, the leader is elected by the Party Council, using the single transferable vote system. Mr Oliver Napier has been leader of the Alliance Party since 1970.

Appendix 1

Principal Minor Parties

This appendix contains a list of those parties which gained at least 1 per cent of the total vote in the constituencies they contested at the general election of May 1979.

Co-operative Party

The Co-operative Party was formed in 1917 and its first MP was elected in 1918, joining the Parliamentary Labour Party in the House of Commons. In 1927 the Co-operative Party reached a formal understanding with the Labour Party, and Co-operative Party branches became eligible for affiliation to Constituency Labour parties. In 1946 an agreement was reached whereby sponsored Co-operative candidates were to run formally as Co-operative and Labour candidates, and in 1959 it was agreed that the number of Co-operative parliamentary candidates should be limited to 30. In the general election of 1979 the Co-operative Party fielded 25 candidates, 17 of whom were elected as MPs.

Ecology Party

The Ecology Party was founded in 1973 after the publication of *Blueprint for Survival*, a work published by the editors of the *Ecologist* magazine, which offered radical proposals for dealing with environmental problems.

In the general election of May 1979 the Ecology Party fielded 50 candidates who together polled 39,918 votes, an average of 1·5 per cent.

National Front

The National Front was formed by a merger of the League of Empire Loyalists and the British National Party in 1967 and was later joined by the Greater Britain Movement. In the general election of May 1979 the National Front fielded 303 candidates who collected 191,791 votes and averaged 1·4 per cent of the vote.

Communist Party

The Communist Party of Great Britain was founded in 1920. In its early years it sought to affiliate with the Labour Party but was turned down, and since 1924 the Labour Party has ruled that no member of the Communist Party can be an individual member of the Labour Party. Throughout its history the Communist Party of Great Britain has returned two members of Parliament—one member was elected for West Fife, Scotland, in 1935 and again in 1945, and another was elected for the Mile End division of Stepney in east London in 1945.

In the general election of May 1979 the Communist Party fielded 38 candidates who between them polled 16,858 votes and gained an average 1·1 per cent of the vote.

ppendix 2

:neral Election Results 1970-79

The table below gives the number of seats won, the number of votes cast and the percentage of votes cast for the various political parties in the four general elections during the period 1970–79. Between the 1970 and February 1974 elections, the number of seats was increased from 630 to 635 as a result of changes in constituency boundaries.

	Seats won	Votes cast	Percentage share of total vote
1970 Election			
Conservative and Associates	330	13,145,123	46·4
Labour	287	12,179,341	43·0
Liberal*	6	2,117,035	7·5
Others†	7	903,299	3·1
1974 (February)			
Labour	301	11,661,657	37·2
Conservative	297†	11,966,481	38·2
Liberal*	14	6,059,519	19·3
Others	23	1,652,505	5·3
1974 (October)			
Labour	319	11,468,618	39·3
Conservative	277†	10,464,799	35·9
Liberal*	13	5,346,704	18·3
Others	26	1,908,983	6·6
1979			
Conservative	339	13,697,753	43·9
Labour	268	11,506,741	36·9
Liberal*	11	4,305,324	13·8
Others†	17	1,712,461	5·4

Source: *The Times Guides to the House of Commons.*

* The number of seats contested by the Liberal Party varied considerably in the elections and this partly accounts for the fluctuations in its vote; the Liberals had 332 candidates in 1970, over 500 in both general elections of 1974 and 577 in 1979. The two main parties normally contest every seat.

† Including the Speaker of the House of Commons. In the two 1974 elections the Speaker, previously a Conservative Member, stood as the Speaker seeking re-election and was opposed by Labour and Liberal candidates. In 1970 and 1979 the Speaker, a former Labour Member, was elected against opposition from independent candidates, but was opposed neither by the Conservative nor by the Liberal Party. On occasions, as in 1959, the Speaker is chosen after the election; on other occasions, as in 1971 and 1976, there has been a change of Speaker between elections.

Party Addresses

The following are the addresses of parties referred to in this pamphlet.

Conservative Party, 32 Smith Square, London SW1P 3HH.

Labour Party, 144–152 Walworth Road, London SE17 1JT.

Social Democratic Party, 4 Cowley Street, London SW1P 3NB.

Liberal Party, 1 Whitehall Place, London SW1A 2HE.

Scottish Liberal Party, 4 Clifton Terrace, Edinburgh EH12 5DR.

Welsh Liberal Party, 15–17 Dumfries Chambers, 91 St Mary's Street, Cardiff CF1 1DW.

Scottish National Party, 6 North Charlotte Street, Edinburgh EH2 4JH.

Plaid Cymru, 51 Cathedral Road, Cardiff CF1 9HD.

Official Unionist Party, 3 Glengall Street, Belfast BT12 5AE.

Democratic Unionist Party, 296 Albertbridge Road, Belfast BT5 49X.

Alliance Party, 88 University Street, Belfast BT7 1HE.

Social Democratic and Labour Party, 38 University Street, Belfast BT7 1FZ.

Co-operative Party, 158 Buckingham Palace Road, London SW1 9UB.

Communist Party, 16 St John Street, London EC1M 4AY.

Ecology Party, 36–38 Clapham Road, London SW9 0JQ.

National Front, 50 Pawson's Grove, Croydon CR0 2QF.

Reading List

BRADLEY, IAN. Breaking the Mould? The Birth and Prospects   £
of the Social Democratic Party.
ISBN 0 85520 469 9.   *Martin Robertson*   1981   8·95

BUTLER, D. *and* KAVANAGH, D. The British General Election of 1979.
ISBN 0 333 26934 9.   *Macmillan*   1980   20·00

COOK, CHRISTOPHER. A Short History of the Liberal Party,
1900–1976. ISBN 0 333 19268 0.   *Macmillan*   1976   3·95

DARBY, JOHN. Conflict in Northern Ireland: The Development
of a Polarised Community.   *Gill and Macmillan*   1976   *Out of print*

LEES, JOHN *and* KIMBER, RICHARD (*ed*). Political Parties in
Modern Britain: An Organisational and Functional Guide.
     Routledge & Kegan Paul   1972   *Out of print*

LINDSAY, T. F. *and* HARRINGTON, MICHAEL. The Conservative
Party 1918–1970. ISBN 0 333 07963 9.   *Macmillan*   1979   5·95

McKENZIE, R. T. British Political Parties. Second edition.
ISBN 0 435 83575 0 (hardback).   *Heinemann*   1964   3·15
ISBN 0 435 83576 9 (paperback).   1·80

PELLING, HENRY. A Short History of the Labour Party.
ISBN 0 333 24435 4.   *Macmillan*   1978   3·95

ROSE, RICHARD. The Problem of Party Government.
ISBN 333 14704 9 (hardback).   *Macmillan*   1974   8·00
ISBN 0 146 21254 4 (paperback).   1976   1·95

The British Parliament. COI reference pamphlet.
ISBN 0 11 701006 5.   *HMSO*   1980   3·80

The Official Opposition in the British Parliament.
COI reference paper, No 180/82.   *COI*   1982

Parliamentary Elections in Britain. COI reference pamphlet.
ISBN 0 11 701039 1.   *HMSO*   1982   2·80

Printed in England for Her Majesty's Stationery Office by Collins & Wilson Ltd., London and Andover
Dd 8333513   C10   2/83

HER MAJESTY'S STATIONERY OFFICE

Government Bookshops

49 High Holborn, London WC1V 6HB
13a Castle Street, Edinburgh EH2 3AR
Brazennose Street, Manchester M60 8AS
Southey House, Wine Street, Bristol BS1 2BQ
258 Broad Street, Birmingham B1 2HE
80 Chichester Street, Belfast BT1 4JY

*Government publications are also available
through booksellers*

£3.15 net

ISBN 0 11 701043 X